من قصص الأنبياء.. في القرآن

Musa

PBUH

مُوسَى

عليه السلام

FROM PROPHETS
STORIES
IN THE QUR'AN

Prepared by:
Dr. Mohamed El Mouelhi

إعداد: د. محمد المويلحي

I0457647

To My Grandchildren, My Inspiration.
-Giddo M.

Text Copyright © 2023 by Mohamed El Mouelhi.
Artwork Copyright © 2023 by Hossam El Mouelhi and Donia Farouk.

All Rights Reserved. No part of this book may be reproduced, transmitted, or stored in an information retrieval system in any form or by any means, graphic, electronic, or mechanical, including photocopying, taping, and recording, without prior written permission from the publisher.
جميع الحقوق محفوظة.
عليه السلام

ISBN 978-1-959536-05-5
First edition 2023

Published by Honey Elm Books LLC
www.HoneyElmBooks.com

Musa PBUH

موسى عليه السلام

Editing: Noha Elmouelhi

Artistic Preparation: Hossam El Mouelhi - Donia Farouk

تحرير: نهى المويلحي

الإعداد الفني: حسام المويلحي– دنيا فاروق

In the Holy Quran,
the name of Prophet Musa (PBUH)
- Allah's prophet to people of Israel
(also known as Children of Israel)-
was mentioned 136 times; this is more than any other
prophet.
Musa was born in Egypt at a time when all newborn boys
among the people of Israel were being killed.
This was because Pharaoh – the king of ancient Egypt –
was afraid that one day someone from the people
of Israel would overthrow him from the throne.
Pharaoh was a cruel ruler who treated the
people of Israel poorly.

1

ورد إسم موسى عليه السلام – نبى الله لبنى إسرائيل – بالقرآن الكريم 136 مرة، وهذا أكثر من أى نبى آخر، وقد ولد موسى عليه السلام بمصر فى وقت كان المواليد الذكور من بنى إسرائيل يقتلونهم لإعتقادهم أن شخصًا منهم سيأتى وسيُلقى فرعون – حاكم مصر – من على عرشه. وكان فرعون حاكمًا جبارًا يسئ معاملة بنى إسرائيل.

His mother was
so afraid for her new baby boy's safety.
Allah revealed to her that she should nurse
him and not to be afraid.
However, she could not hide him for long.
Allah guided her to put Musa in a basket, place the
basket into the Nile River, and that Allah will bring Musa
back to her.

وقد خافت أمه علي حياته بعد ولادته، فأوحى إليها الله أن ترضعه
ولا تخاف عليه، ولكنها لم تستطع الإستمرار فى إخفائه لفترة طويلة، فهداها الله
الى وضع موسى فى سلة وإلقائها فى نهر النيل وأن الله سيرده إليها سالمًا.

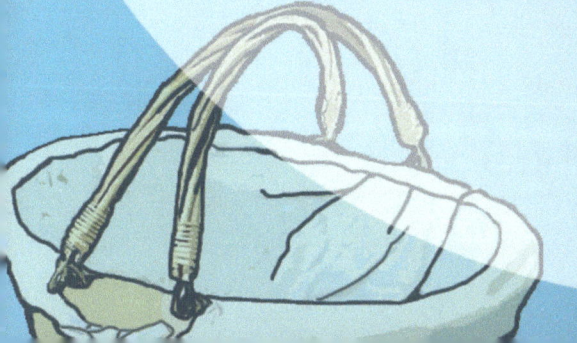

3

Musa's mother put
her baby in a basket and placed it into
the Nile River. The people of Pharaoh found
Musa in the Nile and took him to Pharaoh who was
about to kill him to protect his throne. Allah intervened
and put His Mercy into Pharaoh's wife who pleaded with
Pharaoh to save this baby boy. Pharaoh decided to follow
his wife's wish to raise Musa as their own child.

وضعت أم موسى إبنها الرضيع فى سلة وألقت به فى نهر النيل. ووجده حرس
فرعون وأخذوه الى فرعون ليحكم عليه، ولكن الله وضع رحمته فى قلب
زوجة فرعون فطلبت من زوجها عدم قتل موسى الرضيع لعلهم
يتخذوه ولدًا لهم.

"And We inspired the mother of Musa: `Feed him, but when you fear for him, then cast him into the river and fear not, nor grieve. Verily! We shall bring him back to you, and shall make him one of (Our) Messengers.'" (Al-Qasas:7)

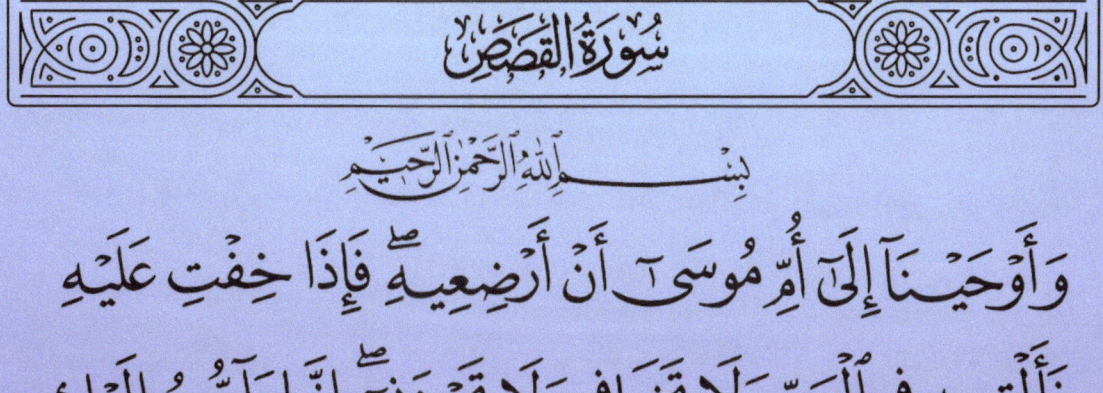

سُورَةُ الْقَصَص

بِسْمِ اللهِ الرَّحْمَٰنِ الرَّحِيمِ

وَأَوْحَيْنَا إِلَىٰ أُمِّ مُوسَىٰ أَنْ أَرْضِعِيهِ ۖ فَإِذَا خِفْتِ عَلَيْهِ فَأَلْقِيهِ فِي الْيَمِّ وَلَا تَخَافِي وَلَا تَحْزَنِي ۖ إِنَّا رَادُّوهُ إِلَيْكِ وَجَاعِلُوهُ مِنَ الْمُرْسَلِينَ ۝

Through the mercy of Allah,
Musa refused to nurse from anyone until
they referred Pharaoh's wife to a lady to nurse him;
this lady was his mother but they were unaware of this
relationship.

Musa was returned to his mother as Allah promised her.
He stayed with his mother for a few years and then went back t
live in Pharaoh's Palace.

Musa grew up to be a knowledgeable, strong and honest man.

ومن رحمة الله أن لم يقبل موسى أيا من المرضعات فى قصر فرعون. فأشاروا
على زوجة فرعون بإحدى المرضعات وقد كانت هذه المرضعة هى أم موسى
ولكن لم يعلم أحد قرابتها للطفل الرضيع، فأرسلوه إليها وأعاده الله لأمه
لترضعه لبضع سنين لتقر عينها، بعد ذلك رجع موسِى لقصر فرعون
وتربى بين فرعون وأسرته، وصاررجلا قويا ونزيهًا
وعلى علم كبير.

6

One day he saw an Egyptian
master in the market fighting with a man from
the people of Israel.
Musa became furious and ran to help the man from
the people of Israel, without realizing his own strength
and accidentally killed the Egyptian master.

وفى يوم من الأيام رأى موسى فى السوق سيدًا مصريًا وآخر من قوم بنى إسرئيل
يتشاجران. فضرب موسى السيد المصرى ضربة قوية دون أن يدرك موسى
مدى قوته فمات السيد المصرى بطريق الخطأ.

Fearing Pharaoh's punishment,
Musa fled to the desert of Madyan (Midian)
located south of Palestine.
After arriving at Madyan, he saw 2 young women
waiting for their turn to fill their water pails from a water
well crowded with men.
He filled up their water pails
and then rested under the shade of a tree.
Musa was very fatigued and not sure what to do after the
accidental death event.
He turned to Allah asking Him for His Bounties in a very beautiful dua.

وبعدها فر موسى هارباً من مصر الى صحراء مدين – الواقعة جنوباً من
فلسطين – خوفا من غضب فرعون وعقابه. وعندما وصل الى مدين وجد
فتاتين تريدان ملأ أوعيتهما من بئر يتزاحم عليه الكثير من الرجال. فساعدهما
موسى وملأ أوعيتهما بالماء ثم جلس فى ظل شجرة ليستريح، وكان
موسى في حالة إرهاق شديد وغير متأكد مما يجب فعله بعد واقعة
القتل الخطأ. فدعا ربه برقة لينعم عليه
ويهديه للخير.

8

"So he watered them,
then he turned back to the shade,
and said: `My Lord! truly, I am in need
of whatever good that You bestow on me!' "
(Al-Qasas: 24)

سُورَةُ القَصَصِ

بِسْمِ اللهِ الرَّحْمَنِ الرَّحِيمِ

فَسَقَىٰ لَهُمَا ثُمَّ تَوَلَّىٰ إِلَى الظِّلِّ فَقَالَ رَبِّ إِنِّى لِمَآ أَنزَلْتَ
إِلَىَّ مِنْ خَيْرٍ فَقِيرٌ ﴿٢٤﴾

Out of Allah's mercy,

He accepted Musa's supplication.

The father of the two young women reassured

Musa and invited him to stay with them. Musa married

one of the 2 young women and spent 10 years in Madyar

إستجاب الله لدعاء موسى إذ إطمأن له كل من والد الفتاتين وإبنتاه، وتزوج
موسى من إحدى الفتاتين ومكث فى مدين عشر سنوات مع أسرته الجديدة.

While traveling with his family,
the greatest event of his life happened to him.
Allah Almighty spoke to Musa at Mount Al-Tur
in Sinai.

Allah ordered him to go back to Egypt to call
on Pharaoh to worship only Allah, and to free
the people of Israel.

وبعد ذلك قرر موسى أن يرحل مع أسرته، وفى الطريق حدث له أعظم حدث
فى حياته إذ كلمه الله عز وجل عند جبل الطور فى سيناء وأمره الله بالعودة
الى مصر لدعوة فرعون وقومه لعبادة الله وإنقاذ بنى إسرائيل من تعذيب
فرعون لهم.

Musa was afraid
of going back alone to Egypt
and confronting Pharaoh.
Allah gave Musa strength to confront Pharaoh
and gave him 2 miracles as evidence
of his true message.
The first miracle turned his walking stick into
a slithering snake.
The second miracle cured his hand from a skin disease
when he placed it in his pocket and took it out.

وكان موسى خائفًا من مقابلة فرعون فطمأنه الله وأنعم عليه بمعجزتين
كدليل على صدق دعوته، وهما عصاه التى تتحول الى ثعبان يسعى
على الارض، والمعجزة الثانية هى يده المصابة بمرض جلدى
والتى تشفى وتصبح ناصعة البياض بوضعها
فى جيبه ثم إخراجها.

12

Musa was still worried
and asked Allah to have his brother
Haroun go with him.
Haroun was a more eloquent speaker and would
be a great source of support to Musa.
Allah granted his wish.

ظل موسى يفكر كيف يقوى على مواجهة فرعون بمفرده، فسأل الله أن
يرسل معه أخاه هارون لكونه أفصح منه وكسند له، فأستجاب الله لطلبه.

Musa and Haroun

went to Pharaoh to deliver Allah's message

and asked him to free the people of Israel.

No one believed them; they all made fun of them.

When Musa showed them the 2 divine miracles, they

called him crazy and a sorcerer.

وذهب موسى وهارون الى فرعون وقومه لتبليغ رسالة الله وطلبا من فرعون
أن يحرر بنى إسرائيل، ولكن قوم فرعون لم يصدقوهما وسخروا منهما، ولما أظهر
موسى معجزتيه من الله إتهموه بالجنون والسحر.

To counter Musa's miracles,
they decided to call all their
great magicians and sorcerers.
The magicians showed great tricks that scared Musa.
Allah assured him and guided him to throw his stick.
It turned into a real snake by the command of Allah and
swallowed all their fake sticks.

وتم تحديد لقاء بين كبار سحرة فرعون وموسى ليتباروا، وجاء السحرة وقاموا بحيل عظيمة أدخلت الخوف في قلب موسى، فطمأنه الله وأمره بإلقاء عصاه على الارض، فإذا هي تنقلب بأمر الله الى ثعبان يأكل ما قام به سحرة فرعون.

15

All of the sorcerers could not believe their eyes and immediately bowed down to the ground.

They now knew that Allah was the only one to be worshiped and no longer feared Pharaoh's punishment and retaliation.

فسجد السحرة وآمنوا بالله وحده غير خائفين من بطش فرعون وتعذيبه لهم.

16

"And throw what you have in your right hand! It will swallow up that which they have made. That which they have made is only a magician's trick, and the magician will never be successful, to whatever amount (of skill) he may attain." (Taha:69)

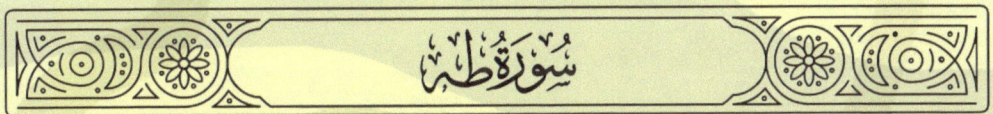

سُورَةُ طه

بِسْمِ اللَّهِ الرَّحْمَنِ الرَّحِيمِ

وَأَلْقِ مَا فِي يَمِينِكَ تَلْقَفْ مَا صَنَعُوٓا۟ إِنَّمَا صَنَعُوا۟ كَيْدُ سَٰحِرٍ وَلَا
يُفْلِحُ السَّاحِرُ حَيْثُ أَتَىٰ ۞

After Pharaoh's magicians were defeated,
Pharaoh punished the people
of Israel even more.
Allah commanded Musa to lead them out
of Egypt and to free them from Pharaoh's torment.

إزداد غضب فرعون بعد هزيمته وخسارة سحرته أمام موسى، فقام بزيادة تعذيبه للذين آمنوا بموسى. وحينذاك أمر الله موسى أن يأخذ بنى إسرائيل لخارج مصر لينجوا من عبودية فرعون وعذابه.

18

**Would Pharaoh
leave the people of Israel
to escape away from him?**

والسؤال الآن:
هل سيترك فرعون بنى إسرائيل أن يفروا
من مملكته؟

19

Of course not!

Pharaoh and his troops were furious
and followed them to kill them.

The people of Israel were scared of Pharaoh,
but Musa assured them that Allah was with them
and would save them.

بالطبع لا! وتبعهم فرعون وجنوده لقتلهم جميعًا، ودب الخوف في قلوب الفارين من بني إسرائيل مع موسى، ولكن موسى أخبرهم أن الله معهم وسينجيهم.

Musa and the people of Israel
fled to the edge of the kingdom
but were trapped as they faced the immense sea
before them.
Pharaoh and his troops were right behind them.

وحين إعترض موسى وبنى إسرائيل البحر فى طريق فرارهم
من فرعون وجنوده. وكان البحر من أمامهم والعدو من خلفهم.

21

Allah revealed to Musa
that he should strike the sea
with his stick to split the sea
and create a path for them to escape.
Musa led the believers through the parted sea safely.

أوحى الله الى موسى أن يضرب البحر بعصاه، فأنشق البحر وأمره الله
أن يمر هو ومن معه من المؤمنين وسط البحر المنشق، ومروا بسلام
للبر الآخر.

Pharaoh and his troops
tried to follow them.

Allah reunited the two sides of the sea
over Pharaoh and his troops and they
all drowned and perished.

وقد حاول فرعون وجنوده اللحاق بهم ولكن الله جعلهم يدخلوا
بين شقى البحر ثم أطبقه عليهم فغرقوا جميعًا.

23

"Then We revealed to Musa:

"Strike the sea with your stick."

And it parted, and each separate part became

like the huge mountain. "

(Al-Shuara: 63)

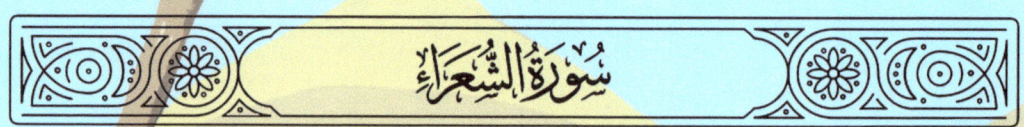

سُورَةُ الشُّعَرَاءِ

بِسْمِ اللَّهِ الرَّحْمَٰنِ الرَّحِيمِ

فَأَوْحَيْنَا إِلَىٰ مُوسَىٰ أَنِ اضْرِب بِّعَصَاكَ الْبَحْرَ ۖ فَانفَلَقَ

فَكَانَ كُلُّ فِرْقٍ كَالطَّوْدِ الْعَظِيمِ ۝

After defeating Pharaoh
and saving the people of Israel,
Musa went to meet Allah. Musa asked to see Allah.
Musa was told by Allah to look at the mountain and to
observe what will happen to the mountain
in front of him once Allah appears to the mountain.
The mountain collapsed completely.
Musa was overwhelmed by this scene and fainted.
After that, Allah revealed His Message (Al-Torah)
to Musa and commanded him to deliver it
to his people.

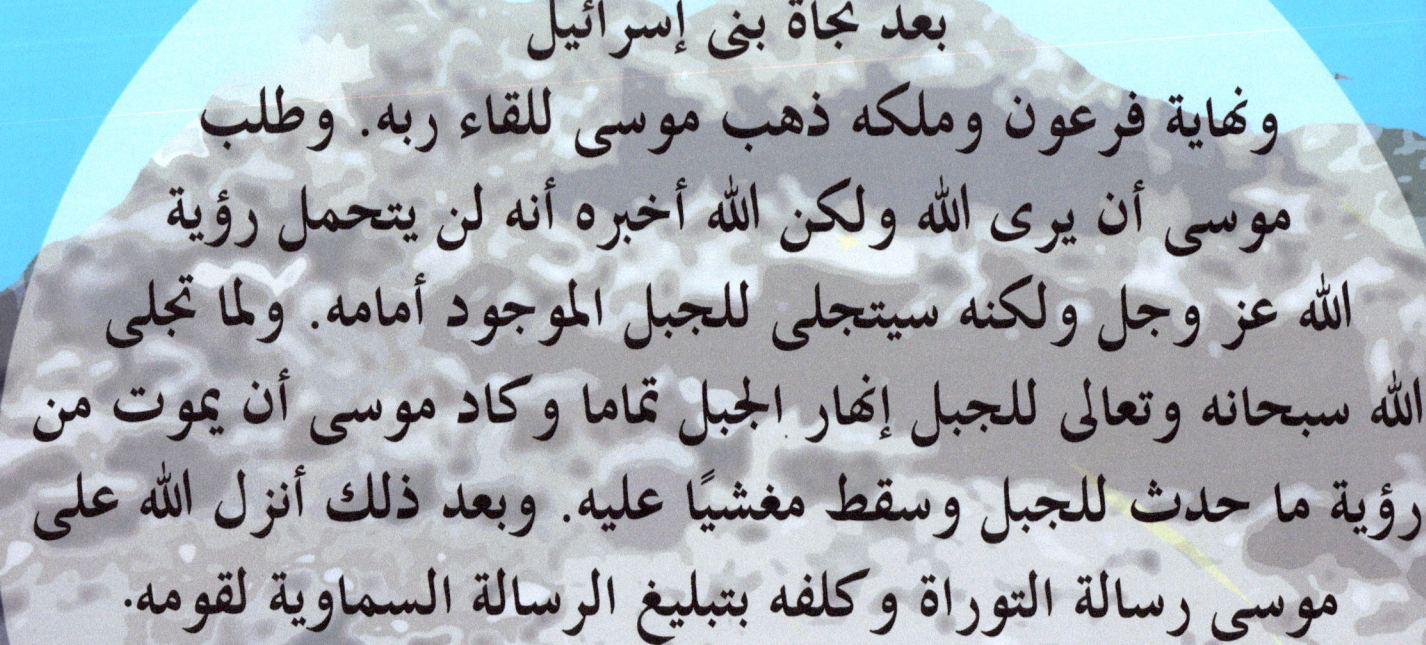

بعد نجاة بني إسرائيل
وبهاية فرعون وملكه ذهب موسى للقاء ربه. وطلب
موسى أن يرى الله ولكن الله أخبره أنه لن يتحمل رؤية
الله عز وجل ولكنه سيتجلى للجبل الموجود أمامه. ولما تجلى
الله سبحانه وتعالى للجبل إنهار الجبل تماما وكاد موسى أن يموت من
رؤية ما حدث للجبل وسقط مغشيًا عليه. وبعد ذلك أنزل الله على
موسى رسالة التوراة وكلفه بتبليغ الرسالة السماوية لقومه.

"he said: `O my Lord! Show me (Yourself),
that I may look upon You.'
Allah said: `You cannot see Me, but look upon the
mountain; if it stands still in its place
then you shall see Me.'
So when Allah appeared to the mountain,
He made it collapse to dust, and Musa
fell down unconscious..."
(Al-Araf:143)

27

بِسْمِ اللَّهِ الرَّحْمَٰنِ الرَّحِيمِ

وَلَمَّا جَاءَ مُوسَىٰ لِمِيقَٰتِنَا وَكَلَّمَهُ رَبُّهُ قَالَ رَبِّ أَرِنِي أَنظُرْ إِلَيْكَ قَالَ لَن تَرَىٰنِي وَلَٰكِنِ ٱنظُرْ إِلَى ٱلْجَبَلِ فَإِنِ ٱسْتَقَرَّ مَكَانَهُ فَسَوْفَ تَرَىٰنِي فَلَمَّا تَجَلَّىٰ رَبُّهُ لِلْجَبَلِ جَعَلَهُ دَكًّا وَخَرَّ مُوسَىٰ صَعِقًا ... ﴿١٤٣﴾

During Musa's absence

to meet Allah, his people went astray

in spite of his brother Haroun's efforts to keep

them on the right path.

One of the people named As-Samiri made a calf

statue out of gold, convinced his people that this golden

calf was their god as well as Musa's god, and the people

began to worship it.

فى أثناء غياب موسى لملاقاة ربه ضل قومه طريقهم على الرغم من جهود أخيه هارون لإستمرارهم فى الطريق الصحيح، فأتبعوا واحدًا منهم — إسمه السامرى — الذى صنع لهم عجلاً من ذهب وأقنعهم أن هذا العجل هو ربهم ورب موسى فقاموا بعبادته.

"Then he produced
for them a calf, which gave forth a lowing sound.
They said: `This is your god,
and the god of Musa, ...' "
(Taha:88)

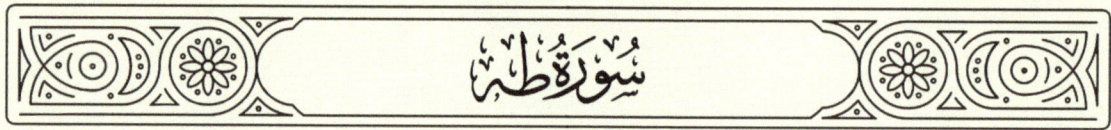
سُورَةُ طٰه

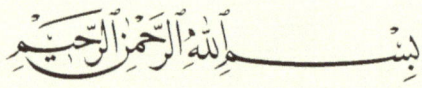
بِسْمِ اللهِ الرَّحْمٰنِ الرَّحِيمِ

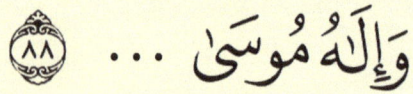
فَأَخْرَجَ لَهُمْ عِجْلًا جَسَدًا لَّهُ خُوَارٌ فَقَالُوا هٰذَا إِلٰهُكُمْ
وَإِلٰهُ مُوسَىٰ ... ﴿٨٨﴾

When Musa returned,
he was angry with his people for abandoning
the worship of Allah Almighty and following
As-Samiri's lie.
Musa continued to be patient and guided them back to
the way of Allah.

ولما رجع موسى الى قومه غضب لتركهم عبادة الله الواحد
وإتباعهم أكذوبة السامرى. ولما ذهب عنه الغضب بدأ موسى بتبليغ
رسالة التوراة لقومه وتوجيههم إلى عبادة الله سبحانه وتعالى.

The way of Allah

Musa was a strong
and knowledgeable person.
But Allah wanted to show him that there
is always someone more knowledgeable.
Allah commanded Musa to follow another righteous
knowledgeable person - Al-Khidr - to learn from him.
When they met, Al-Khidr stipulated that Musa should
not ask him about the things that he does until he explains
them to him.

كان موسى رجلا قوياً وذا علم، ولكن الله أراد أن يعلمه أن
هناك من هو أعلم منه. حدث ذلك عندما قابل موسى رجلاً
تقيًا يدعى الخضر والذى صاحبه للتعلم منه، وإشترط
الخضر على موسى ألا يسأله عن أشياء يقوم بها
أثناء رحلتهم حتى يشرحها له.

During their journey,
Musa twice asked Al-Khidr
why he was doing things.
Al-Khidr kept reminding him of their agreement
– wait until I explain to you
the reason behind my actions.
Then, Musa said if I ask a third time, then it will be
the end of our companionship.

وفى أثناء رحلتهما سأل موسى الخضر مرتين وذكّره
الخضر بإتفاقهما، وبعدها تعهد له موسى ألا يصاحبه إذا سأله
عن شئ بعد ذلك.

They passed by a village
that its people refused to host them
or offer them food.
When they found an old wall about to collapse,
Al-Khidr went ahead and fixed it.
Musa at this point asked Al-Khidr why he fixed the wall
for free for people who refused to host them.

ومرا بقرية وكانا جياعًا ولكن أهل القرية رفضوا إطعامهما
وإستضافتهما، ورأى الخضر حائطًا قديمًا على وشك الإنهيار
فقام بإصلاحه. عندها لم يتمالك موسى نفسه وسأل الخضر
لماذا قام بإصلاح الحائط بلا أى مقابل لقوم
رفضوا إستضافتهم.

Al-Khidr informed Musa
that this broken wall belonged
to orphans in town and underneath
it was a treasure left by their deceased father
who was a righteous person.
Allah wanted to save the children's inheritance
until they grew up; Al-Khidr was just following Allah's
Command.

أخبر الخضر موسى أن تحت هذا الحائط كنز لأطفال يتامى
تركه لهم أبوهم المتوفى والذى كان رجلًا صالحًا، فأراد الله
المحافظة على هذا الكنز الى أن يكبر الأطفال
ويستخرجوه، وأنه كان ينفذ أمر الله.

35

As this was the third time
that Musa could not be patient enough
to wait for an explanation,
it was the end of Musa's journey with Al-Khidr.

وكانت هذه هى نهاية رحلة موسى مع الخضر لعدم صبره
حتى يخبره الخضر عن سبب ما كان يعمل.

MUSA'S LIFE AND HIS JOURNEY WITH AL-KHIDR HAVE MANY LESSONS TO REMEMBER:

- Remember to be humble and stay away from arrogance, regardless of our knowledge, wealth, or social status.

- Be patient and don't rush things. Many unusual things happen to us in life, but at a later time we discover their reason and great value.

- Our knowledge is limited; there is always room to learn more.

- Good deeds are never wasted but remain for the next generation.

- We all make mistakes. We must learn from them and try to better ourselves and seek Allah's help to return to the right path.

37

قصة موسى عليه السلام
ورحلته مع الخضر فيها عدة دروس مستفادة:

-التواضع والبعد عن الغرور مهما كان علمنا أو ثراءنا أو وضعنا الإجتماعي.

-التحلى بالصبر وعدم التسرع، فهناك أشياء غريبة تحدث لنا فى حياتنا ويتضح لنا فى وقت لاحق سببها وفائدتها الكبرى.

-درجة معرفتنا محدودة، وهناك دائما فرصة لتعلم أشياء جديدة.

-العمل الصالح لا يضيع بل يُحفظ للأجيال التالية.

-كلنا نرتكب أخطاء، ويجب أن نتعلم منها ونحاول تحسين أنفسنا ونستعين بالله في العودة إلى الطريق الصحيح.

MUSA'S WALKING STICK PLAYED MANY ROLES IN HIS LIFE, CAN YOU NAME 2 OF THEM?

لعبت عصا موسى عليه السلام أدوار عديدة فى حياته ، هل يمكنك ذكر إثنين منها؟

39

Among the roles played
by Musa's walking stick in his life:

* As one of the miracles to help Musa deliver
Allah's message: his walking stick turned into a slithering snake.

* Allah revealed to Musa that he should strike the sea with his
walking stick to part the sea and create a path for Musa and his people
to escape from Pharoah and his troops.

من الأدوار التى لعبتها عصا موسى فى حياته:

*إحدى المعجزات كدليل على صدق دعوته أن تحولت العصا الى ثعبان يسعى
على الارض.

* أوحى اللّه الى موسى أن يضرب البحر بعصاه، فأنشق البحر
لينجوا موسى ومن آمن معه من فرعون وجنوده.

Musa PBUH

is one of the Prophets

in the Quran.

Allah revealed to him

the Torah, and he was the owner

of the walking stick

with many uses.

موسى عليه السلام
هو أحد الأنبياء
فى القرآن، أنزل الله
عليه "التوراة"، وصاحب العصا
متعددة الأغراض.

41

Watch a special reading of Musa PBUH by the author!

Scan this QR code to access the video.

www.ingramcontent.com/pod-product-compliance
Lightning Source LLC
Chambersburg PA
CBHW041555120626
46551CB00002B/210